I0111993

Unmasking
THE
ROARING
LION

McDougal & Associates
Servants of Christ and Stewards of the
Mysteries of God

Unmasking
THE
ROARING
LION

Jane P. McCoy

Published by:

McDougal & Associates
18896 Greenwell Springs Road
Greenwell Springs, LA 70739

www.ThePublishedWord.com

McDougal & Associates is an organization dedicated to the spreading of the Gospel of the Lord Jesus Christ to as many people as possible in the shortest time possible.

ISBN: 978-1-950398-14-0

Printed in the U.S., the U.K. and Australia
For Worldwide Distribution

Dedication

I dedicate this book to the Lord, who is the center of my life. May His name be praised and glorified as this book brings His people a life of healing and liberation. To the God Who is Love.

Contents

FOR GOD HATH NOT GIVEN US
THE SPIRIT OF FEAR; BUT OF
POWER, AND OF LOVE, AND OF A
SOUND MIND.
2 Timothy 1:7

Introduction

Fear is rapidly becoming a household occupant of many families throughout the world. Although we are faced with many challenges and uncertainties, national and international threats, environmental threats, wars, murders, abductions and diseases, a child of God is commanded not to fear.

Fear is not of God. Therefore, we must resist it. We must resist anything that is not of Him. In these last and evil days, we must draw closer to God. We have hope and confidence in Him and in His Word.

> *Submit yourselves therefore unto God. Resist the devil, and he will flee from you.*
>
> James 4:7

As children of God, we take refuge in Him and His promises.

Unmasking the Roaring Lion

In this book, we will learn how Satan, our adversary, has tormented and is still tormenting the children of God, and fear is one of his favorite tools. But fear is a foe that should never be tolerated in the Christian life. Fear, as an agent of Satan, has an assignment. We will uncover the plans of the enemy through fear. We will learn to recognize fear, we will learn what it looks like, what it sounds like and what it feels like.

Fear is like a roaring lion. Lions roars often and for different reasons. They roar particularly before the sun rises and at sunset and, by doing so, they make the environment of their prey uncomfortable. That is exactly how fear works on us.

My prayer is that after you have completed this book, the God of Peace, Jehovah Shalom, will have visited you with deliverance from all fear. God bless and deliver you as you read and study *Unmasking the Roaring Lion*.

Jane P. McCoy

CHAPTER 1

Fear and Its Design

For God hath not given us the spirit of fear;
but of power, and of love, and of a sound mind.
2 Timothy 1:7

There are two types of fear. One of them is a healthy fear, one that will protect us from danger and trouble. The other fear is a destructive fear, one that keeps us from moving forward in life. It paralyzes us, debilitating us to the point of inactivity—psychologically and physiologically.

In this book, we will focus on the negative impact fear can have on our lives and how it causes a rift in our relationships and wreaks havoc on our daily lives, eventually taking its toll on our mental and physical health. Fear hinders our relationship with God and with others, and fear will keep us from the fulfillment of our God-given destiny. God says that He has not given us this spirit called fear.

What is this thing called fear? *Fear (G1167; di-lee'ah)*, "timidity; fear" (from G1169; *di-los*), "dread; timid, that is, by implication faithless; fearful."

We know that fear is a spirit, and that it was not sent to us by God. And anything not sent by God is not good, but evil and wicked.

James wrote to the churches:

> *Every good gift and every perfect gift is from above, and cometh down from the Father of lights, with whom is no variableness, neither shadow of turning.* James 1:17

We have an adversary, the devil, and he is seeking to devour our lives and our destiny. The apostle Peter warned us in the Scriptures:

> *Be sober, be vigilant; because your adversary the devil, as a roaring lion, walketh about, seeking whom he may devour.* 1 Peter 5:8

In this life, we will be faced with uncertainties, perilous confrontations, wars, etc., but God has promised to deliver us out of them all:

Fear and Its Design

Many are the afflictions of the righteous: but the
LORD delivereth him out of them all.

Psalm 34:19

Affliction: (H7451; *rah, raw-aw'*), "adversity, affliction, bad, calamity; distress," from the root (H7489;
raw-ah') "to spoil literally by breaking to pieces; good
for nothing, bad (physically, socially or morally)."
By definition, the enemy seeks to destroy us.

Today we are surrounded by life issues which
threaten our safety, hope and even our faith. We are
no different than the children of Israel when they
were delivered to serve the Almighty. God Himself
brought them through many perilous and question-
able situations. God always spoke and assured them
of this one thing: He would not leave them to the
hands of the enemy:

And the LORD, he it is that doth go before thee;
he will be with thee, he will not fail thee, neither
forsake thee: fear not, neither be dismayed.

Deuteronomy 31:8

Jehovah goes before His people, to seek out a place
of rest for them. He is faithful and will not fail us.

Unmasking the Roaring Lion

Neither will He leave us. He cautions us not to be depressed, disappointed, shocked or disgusted.

David was so confident in the promises of God that he penned the words of Psalm 23:4:

> *Yea, though I walk through the valley of the shadow of death, I will fear no evil: for thou art with me; thy rod and thy staff they comfort me.*

David had learned to trust and depend on God through it all, even during life-threatening circumstances.

Paul also trusted in God when he was faced with dire circumstances. He wrote:

> *For we would not, brethren, have you ignorant of our trouble which came to us in Asia, that we were pressed out of measure, above strength, insomuch that we despaired even of life: but we had the sentence of death in ourselves, that we should not trust in ourselves, but in God which raiseth the dead: who delivered us from so great a death, and doth deliver: in whom we trust that he will yet deliver us.*
>
> 2 Corinthians 1:8-10

Fear and Its Design

Some of us are faced with dreadful situations day after day and even for many months or years. Jehovah is the God of Light. He lightens our situations. It is He who carries the load with us, for He is our Burden Bearer.

God will never give you more than you can bear. Your situations will not overtake you ... unless you give in to them. Do not fear the darkness of this moment:

> *The LORD is my light and my salvation; whom shall, I fear? The LORD is the strength of my life; of whom shall I be afraid?* Psalm 27:1

Yes, whom?

It gives me great comfort in the midst of trouble to know that God is bigger than any of my troubles, and He is sovereign over all things that come to my life.

Prayer, praise and thanksgivings are the antidotes for fear:

> *At what time I am afraid, I will trust in thee. In God I will praise his word, in God I have put my trust; I will not fear what flesh can do unto me.* Psalm 56:3-4

Fear would have you doubt every promise of God that rightfully belongs to you. The enemy comes to rob, kill and destroy your hope in God.

When we pray about everything, it keeps us from worrying or being anxious. Therefore, the Scriptures command us to pray about everything, doubting nothing. We must make our request known to God. And when we pray, we must believe that God has already answered and, therefore, in return, we give thanks for what we are assured is to come. This assurance will keep us from fears, frustrations and anxieties:

> *And the peace of God, which passeth all understanding, shall keep your hearts and minds through Christ Jesus.*   Philippians 4:7

A little voice in your head may be asking, "But how long should I pray?" Jesus taught us:

> *Men ought always to pray, and not to faint.*
> Luke 18:1

So we should continue to pray until something happens.

Fear and Its Design

In our prayers, we need not use *"vain repetitions,"* but we should be diligent in prayer for all men everywhere.

Is God deaf that He cannot hear us? No:

I sought the Lord, and he heard me, and delivered me from all my fears. Psalm 34:4

Every day we hear news of wars, killings, child abductions, etc., and all of this can cause us to walk in fear ... that is if we are not confident in the promises of God. Some of those things are happening all around us in our own communities, and the result is that we often see no way out. But Jesus is the way out of fear. Perfect love casts out all fear. Of this, we are assured:

There is no fear in love; but perfect love casteth out fear: because fear hath torment. He that feareth is not made perfect in love.

1 John 4:18

Again we see that fear causes a person to be tormented. We will discuss the consequences of fear in another section.

Today people around the world are struggling with illnesses which so far have no cure. We experience epidemics and no knowledge of how they came about. Therefore we don't know the course to take in their prevention. These things are known as *"terrors of the night."*

> *You shall not be afraid of the terror of the night, nor of the arrow (the evil plots and slanders of the wicked) that flies by day.*
>
> Psalm 91:5, AMPC

Does all of this give us reasons for concern? Of course, it does, but we are not to be haunted because of any of these things. Jehovah watches over us as a hen watches over her chicks. He keeps us hidden in a secret place. In God, there is a place of security, assurance and rest. He said:

> *He that dwelleth in the secret place of the most High shall abide under the shadow of the Almighty.*
>
> Psalm 91:1

That secret place is in His presence, in the Person of Christ Jesus. If you have chosen Christ as Lord and Savior over your life, then He is your Dwelling Place, your Hiding Place. You are hid in Christ Jesus:

> *For ye are dead, and your life is hid with Christ in God.* Colossians 3:3

God Himself has raised us up and has made us to sit together in heavenly places in Christ Jesus. We have the certainty of security:

> *The name of the LORD is a strong tower: the righteous runneth into it and is safe.*
> Proverb 18:10

"So, why are we so fearful?" we ask ourselves. When the unfortunate events of life happen to us and we lack the knowledge of God and His promises, it can cause us to walk in fear and not faith. He said:

> *My people are destroyed for lack of knowledge: because thou hast rejected knowledge, I will also reject thee, that thou shalt be no priest to me: seeing thou hast forgotten the law of thy God, I will also forget thy children.* Hosea 4:6

Those who lack the knowledge of God are in serious trouble. Fear keeps them bound and in captivity.

Captivity: (H1540, *gaw-law*) "denude; strip (something) of its covering, possessions, or assets, especially it a disgraceful sense." God declared through Isaiah:

> *Therefore my people are gone into captivity, because they have no knowledge: and their honourable men are famished, and their multitude dried up with thirst.*   Isaiah 5:13

When we lack knowledge, we suffer because of it, and it is the Word of God that gives us the necessary knowledge:

> *Wisdom is the principal thing; therefore, get wisdom: and with all thy getting get understanding.*   Proverbs 4:7

We are required to ask, seek and knock for the wisdom of God. It's in the seeking that we find, in the knocking that revelation will be given to us, and in the asking that we will gain the wisdom of God.

Fear and Its Design

As believers in Christ, we are all required to study the Word of God:

> *Study to shew thyself approved unto God, a workman that needeth not to be ashamed, rightly dividing the word of truth.*
>
> 2 Timothy 2:15

As we seek the truth of God, fear will no longer have dominion over us.

Fear paralyzes us, making us think we are alone, helpless and defeated, but the prophet Isaiah assured us that we are *not* alone:

> *Fear thou not; for I am with thee: be not dismayed; for I am thy God: I will strengthen thee; yea, I will help thee; yea, I will uphold thee with the right hand of my righteousness.*
>
> Isaiah 41:10

Jesus gave us this same assurance:

> *Lo, I am with you always, even unto the end of the world. Amen.*
>
> Matthew 28:20

It is the Father's will that no harm should come to a child of God:

> *But even the very hairs of your head are all numbered. Fear not therefore: ye are of more value than many sparrows.* Luke 12:7

Yes, we are worth far more than a bird in God's sight, for we are made in His very image.

Eventually, the spirit of fear, if allowed to remain long enough in us, will make us sick. God is not only interested in healing us; His desire is to keep us free from infectious diseases, keeping us from many concerns, and from a long list of psychosomatic diseases that are increasing despite all of the efforts of modern medicine.

Psychosomatic means "1. a physical illness or other condition caused or aggravated by a material factor such as internal conflict or stress. 2. Relating to the interaction of mind and body." The Scriptures clearly assert that God is concerned about our entirety—body, soul and spirit.

> *And the very God of peace sanctify you wholly; and I pray God your whole spirit and soul and*

body be preserved blameless unto the coming of our Lord Jesus Christ. 1 Thessalonians 5:23

Wholly (G3651; *holoteles'*) "to complete to the end, absolutely perfect."

Soul (G5590; *psoo-khay'*) "breath, that is (by implication) spirit, abstractly or concretely; comprised of the (mind, thought, intellect)."

Body (G4982; *so'-mah)* "the body as a sound whole."

On a personal level, I suffered from allergies in the past and didn't understand why. As I began my journey toward healing, my way of thinking about diseases needed to change. Sinus allergies ruled over me for a period until I learned how to be free of them.

I witnessed my late mother going through this same agony. The more I sought God the more I became convinced that my own condition was somehow rooted in something unclean or an inherited disease. Now that I know sinus has a spiritual root (fear, anxiety and abuse), I know there is a need to first deal with the psychological (mind) issues before the physiological (physical or body) issues can be corrected. This is what has driven me to share this book and to enlighten others to the fact that fear, anxiety and stress can negatively impact our lives.

Unmasking the Roaring Lion

I pray that this book will help you to recognize the false god behind fear. Knowing the enemy and his game plan is half of the battle. I pray that you will also be set free from the bondage of fear and be able to stand fast in the liberty that is in Christ:

> *Stand fast therefore in the liberty wherewith Christ hath made us free, and be not entangled again with the yoke of bondage.*
>
> Galatians 5:1

May God set you free from the bondage of fear, in Jesus' name.

CHAPTER 2

Fear Is Not from God

For God hath not given us the spirit of fear;
but of power, and of love, and of a sound mind.
2 Timothy 1:7

1. *Fear* (G1167; *di-lech'ah*) "timidity," from (G1169; *di-los'*) "dread; timid, that is (by implication) faithless; fearful."

2. *Timidity*: 1. "lacking in courage or self-confidence, 2. Lacking in boldness or determination."

3. *Dread*; 1. "to fear greatly, 2. To feel extreme reluctance to meet or face. a. A great fear especially in the face of impending evil. b. extreme uneasiness in face of disagreeable prospects; exposure."

Timothy was a young bishop in the church at Ephesus, and young people can often be intimidated by their elders for various reasons. One reason Timothy might have been intimidated was the maturity of some elder saints in the very thing God had commanded Timothy to teach. He had been given detailed instructions on how he should run the church, but it had mature saints in it, and it was a large church. This must have been very challenging for Timothy because it was his first assignment as a bishop.

We know that anytime a newcomer shows up with proposed changes, we resist that person and the changes he or she wants to bring into our midst. People resist change, to the point of rebelling and causing others to rebel. Nevertheless, when we have a job to do, we cannot allow the faces and voices of men to deter us from accomplishing the will of God.

Did Paul think Timothy could do the job? Certainly. Timothy had been trained in the Word from a child by his mother and grandmother. Paul reminded Timothy of this as an encouragement to him:

> *When I call to remembrance the unfeigned faith that is in thee, which dwelt first in thy grandmother Lois, and thy mother Eunice; and I am persuaded that in thee also.*   2 Timothy 1:5

Fear Is Not from God

Apparently Timothy was having issues with the negative effects of fear, and Paul needed to remind him what he was made of. As we have noted, fear can paralyze us.

Let us examine this word *paralyze* and its effects. *Paralyze:* "to make powerless and ineffective. Unnerve; to deprive of courage and strength." By definition, what Timothy was expected to accomplish was impossible without continuous encouragement and affirmation from Paul.

In the same way, I encourage you to take heart. Fears that cripple us are not of God. God has called you to be productive in this earth and to subdue it. Fear will make you feel as if you are useless and unable to effectively do your God-given assignment.

On our jobs, some have to face employers who rule with a rod of iron. The employee, gripped by fear, becomes nervous and upset at the presence of the boss, and the result is ineffectiveness. When the boss is away, that same employee may complete the job in a timely and efficient manner.

Fear will make you feel inferior, inadequate and ineffective. This spirit is robbing you of, 1). Your peace, 2.) Your health, 3). Your identity, 4). Your prosperity and 5). Your purpose. Fear keeps us from being the people God called us to be.

The fear of man bringeth a snare: but whoso putteth his trust in the LORD shall be safe.

Proverbs 29:25

Paralyze speaks of a complete or partial loss of function, especially when involving the motion or sensation in any part of the body. Remember, fear is activated in the mind and then effects the physical body. This lets me know that fear will first attack your mind. It distorts your thinking:

I'm not good enough.
I can't do this:
I'm not fit for this.
I'm just not capable of doing what you want me to do.
Let someone else do this; they could do a better job than I can.

At times, we actually just sit idly by and don't do anything—all as a result of fear. But these are all lies. If you believe these things, it is because you have been gripped by fear and its negative effects.

Fear will come over you without warning, as a surprise, as a trap. Just like a deer caught in the headlights, you will be frozen and unable to move or defend yourself. In that moment of helplessness, fear will flood your mind with thoughts of defeat, doubt, and immobility. Fear will make you run from place to place in an attempt to escape its accusations:

> *Therefore snares are round about thee, and sudden fear troubleth thee; or darkness, that thou canst not see; and abundance of waters cover thee.*   Job 22:10-11

The mind begins to wander, feeling overcome and defeated, and looking for some means of escape. You might even use the various methods of escape—drugs, alcohol, sex or food. But, in the end, fear is still there, lingering and disrupting your life.

God wants the Church to get involved with the healing of those affected and infected by fear, and the Scriptures give us clear precepts of what to do whenever one is sick among us. Unfortunately, many in today's church don't want much to do with sickness outside of offering a capsule. But the ministry of Jesus Christ, our Great Example, was healing the sick, binding up the wounded and setting captives free. And the commission He has given us has not changed. We ought to be about our Father's business, and part of that is bringing healing to those who have been negatively affected by the enemy.

James wrote:

> *Is any sick among you? let him call for the elders of the church; and let them pray over him, anointing him with oil in the name of the Lord: and the prayer of faith shall save the sick, and the Lord shall raise him up; and if he have committed sins, they shall be forgiven him. Confess your faults one to another, and pray one for another, that ye may be healed. The effectual fervent prayer of a righteous man availeth much.*   James 5:14-16

Fear doesn't just affect the mind (*psyche'*); it also affects the body (*soma*). Once the spirit of fear takes control of the mind, intellect, will and emotions (through the brain), it then controls what happens with the body through the function of glands and hormones. The limbic system affects the emotions, our behavior, our motivation, our long-term memory and even our olfaction or sense of smell. I'm not a doctor, but I have learned this much through my research. And through it, I have been set free from fear and its control over my life.

Fear Is Not from God

Fear is a very effective tool used by that old Serpent, the Dragon, the devil, and it may have gained access to your life. It is not just an emotion, as many think. Fear that comes at a debilitating level is an evil spirit, and any spirit that is not of God is an evil spirit. Remember, *"God hath not given us the spirit of fear."*

What do we do in the face of fear? Jehoshaphat, King of Judah, was a righteous man. He walked after the ways of the Lord his God, and the Lord commended him through the prophet:

> *Nevertheless, there are good things found in thee, in that thou hast taken away the groves out of the land, and hast prepared thine heart to seek God.* 2 Chronicles 19:3

In this 19th chapter of 2 Chronicles, we can see how this godly king set reform in place. He tore down idols and appointed the Levites, the priests and the chief of the elders in their respective places, to hear and judge any and every controversy:

> *And he charged them, saying, Thus shall ye do in the fear of the LORD, faithfully, and with a perfect heart.* 2 Chronicles 19:9

However, walking in the fear of God and being a good person doesn't exempt you from suffering afflictions, conflicts and wars. After a time of peace, Jehoshaphat was suddenly threatened with war. The Ammonites, who opposed reform, and the Moabites, with their perverted mentality, came against the king to do battle. The matter was made worse when messengers kept coming with the same repeated threats. The Scriptures tell us:

> *And Jehoshaphat feared, and set himself to seek the LORD, and proclaimed a fast throughout all Judah. And Judah gathered themselves together, to ask help of the LORD: even out of all the cities of Judah they came to seek the LORD.*
>
> 2 Chronicles 20:3-4

The word *feared* (H3372; *yaw-ray*) means "frighten, make afraid, dread." The definition of *dread*, according to the *New Oxford American Dictionary* is "anticipate with great apprehension or fear. Fear, be afraid, worry about, be anxious about, forebodings about, shrink from."

This king had loads of hormones dumping into his blood stream, and fear set off an alarm, fright or flight. Fortunately for Jehoshaphat, he made a good decision in that moment. He would stand up to the enemy by seeking the face of the Lord:

> *At what time I am afraid I will trust the Lord.*
> Psalm 56:3

The king trusted God and sought Him through prayer and fasting and did not allow the enemy to win this battle. God responded to Jehoshaphat's prayers and fought the battle for him and his people.

Gideon was another man chosen by God to bring deliverance to Israel. When God called him, he was hiding in a winepress threshing wheat (to hide it from the Amalekites). The Lord sees and knows all things, and yet His salutation to Gideon went like this:

> *And the angel of the Lord appeared unto him,*
> *and said unto him, The Lord is with thee, thou*
> *mighty man of valour.* Judges 6:12

The Lord didn't judge Gideon in his current situation of fear. Instead, He addressed Gideon as He had purposed him. He saw Gideon as fulfilling his destiny as a deliverer of Israel.

Then the Lord gave Gideon the opportunity to face fear head-on. Gideon's father was an idol worshipper, a devotee of Baal, and he had an altar and a grove in his backyard. This was Gideon's opportunity:

> *And it came to pass the same night, that the* Lord *said unto him, Take thy father's young bullock, even the second bullock of seven years old, and throw down the altar of Baal that thy father hath, and cut down the grove that is by it: and build an altar unto the* Lord *thy God upon the top of this rock, in the ordered place, and take the second bullock, and offer a burnt sacrifice with the wood of the grove which thou shalt cut down.* Judges 6:25-26

The destruction of the second bullock signified establishment. There was to be no more idolatry in the land. By Gideon's actions, he was saying, " I will serve no other god but Jehovah."

Gideon accept his God-given assignment, but not without having to face fear. The Scriptures say, *"he feared"* (H3372). This time, Gideon sought the help and support of others:

Fear Is Not from God

Then Gideon took ten men of his servants, and did as the LORD had said unto him: and so it was, because he feared his father's household, and the men of the city, that he could not do it by day, that he did it by night. And when the men of the city arose early in the morning, behold, the altar of Baal was cast down, and the grove was cut down that was by it, and the second bullock was offered upon the altar that was built. Judges 6:27-28

Gideon gained victory over his fears by placing his trust in Jehovah. After the Lord confirmed and assured him that He would be with him, his confidence grew, and he refused to allow fear to paralyze him, make him feel inadequate, inferior or useless. Gideon was encouraged by his encounter with the Lord. The Lord spoke life, potential and greatness into the life of Gideon. We, too, ought to also encourage one another with words that edify and not destroy. Our speech should always be seasoned to the hearer, seasoned so that our words can preserve, heal and transform lives:

Let your speech be always with grace, seasoned with salt, that ye may know how ye ought to answer every man. Colossians 4:6

We are the salt of the earth:

Ye are the salt of the earth: but if the salt have lost his savour, wherewith shall it be salted? it is thenceforth good for nothing, but to be cast out, and to be trodden under foot of men. Matthew 5:13

These two men, Jehoshaphat and Gideon, are great examples of how we should manage fear. Not everyone is so successful in their attempts. Fear is an emotion, and when we give in to it, it causes not only spiritual problems, but also physical problems. Nevertheless, God will help us and lead us into victory when we commit our ways to Him.

Then he answered and spake unto me, saying, This is the word of the LORD unto Zerubbabel, saying, Not by might, nor by power, but by my spirit, saith the LORD of hosts. Zechariah 4:6

Fear Is Not from God

In Genesis 3, we read that Adam, the son of God, hid himself from his Creator because he was frightened, after having disobeyed the command of God. Disobedience to God and His commands will make us feel guilty and ashamed of our actions. All too often, the result is that we try desperately to hide from God. Such a breach presents an opening to evil. Evil thoughts had now gripped Adam and determined how he saw God:

> *And he said, I heard thy voice in the garden, and I was afraid, because I was naked; and I hid myself.*
> *And he said, Who told thee that thou wast naked? Hast thou eaten of the tree, whereof I commanded thee that thou shouldest not eat?*
>
> Genesis 3:10-11

Adam was afraid, and this also made him blame others for his disobedience. Fear will have us to look for excuses for our failure and run for cover. In an attempt to hide the consequences of their rebellion, Adam and Eve sewed fig leaves together to cover themselves.

God asked Adam who had told him he was naked, and had he eaten from the tree which he was com-

manded not to eat of. Adam responded by blaming
God for putting him in such a predicament:

> *And the man said, The woman whom thou*
> *gavest to be with me, she gave me of the tree,*
> *and I did eat.* Genesis 3:12

God is gracious and full of mercy. When we sin,
we have an Advocate with the Father, Jesus Christ.
Jesus Christ and His atoning blood are still at work
today. When we sin, we are to confess our faults and
apply His atoning blood to cover that sin:

> *If we confess our sins, he is faithful and just to*
> *forgive us our sins, and to cleanse us from all*
> *unrighteousness.* 1 John 1:9

We have a way back to the Father through the
Son. Fear will make you run, but love will cover
you and restore you back to the Father. Love covers
and make things complete, whereas fear makes you
afraid, ashamed and feeling guilty and causes you
to separate from God's love.

Abraham, in Genesis 20, lied, saying that Sarah
was his sister, when she was his wife. Feeling infe-

rior to those in the land, Abraham lied because he feared for his life. Abraham recognized the voice of God and obeyed Him, but he didn't trust God completely. In that moment of intimidation by people in an unfamiliar land, he failed God.

Abraham's actions placed Sarah and her divine purpose at risk. Sarah was appointed to bring forth Isaac, the son of promise, through whose bloodline the Messiah would come. God intervened for Abraham and Sarah and visited Abimelech in a dream, to protect His divine plan for Sarah:

> *But God came to Abimelech in a dream by night, and said to him, Behold, thou art but a dead man, for the woman which thou hast taken; for she is a man's wife.* Genesis 20:3

We must remember God in all things—no matter the people around us, their ways, the differences in culture or the sound of their roar.

Fear will cause us to put our divine purpose in jeopardy and sometimes overthrow that destiny. In the face of fear, we must look to God and His promises. He promises to deliver us from all fears, but we must do our part:

Unmasking the Roaring Lion

> *Be sober, be vigilant; because your adversary the*
> *devil, as a roaring lion, walketh about, seeking*
> *whom he may devour.* 1 Peter 5:8

We must not fear the roar of the enemy.

Fear itself, being a messenger of Satan, will try to motivate us to work the works of darkness—lies, intimidation and manipulation. When we are controlled and motivated by darkness, our motives are no longer pure:

> *For ye were sometimes darkness, but now are*
> *ye light in the Lord: walk as children of light.*
> Ephesians 5:8

Both Adam and Abraham are examples left for us. The ways of God are always righteous. We can totally trust Him. In our falling and our failures, He is there to ransom us. He places a hedge around us to protect His purpose and plans. He will never leave us nor forsake us. Therefore, fear not!

Where does fear come from? It can come from the presence of a handicap. It can come from a condition that restricts your ability to function (for example, a

Fear Is Not from God

lack of education, your age, your financial position, your physical makeup, your ethnicity). It can come from the persistence of our doubts, which are really the voice of Satan himself. He is saying:

- You will never make it!
- You have failed before!
- No one in your family has amounted to anything!
- You are not nearly good enough!
- You will never defeat the enemy!
- You have no support!
- Too much is being expected of you!
- You are expecting way too much!
- This is such a huge responsibility!
- Everyone is pushing you to succeed, regardless of the cost!
- If you don't make it, people will laugh at you!
- Other people have favor, but not you!
- The pressure from your opposition is too great!
- Your opponents have the ability to manipulate others, but you don't!
- God is such a fool!

Unmasking the Roaring Lion

Fear can enter through a broken spirit. A broken spirit can happen when one is rejected, abandoned or betrayed. Rejection causes fear because there is a feeling of being unloved, not being important, not being needed, not being accepted, etc. When this happens, a person may develop feelings of insecurity. Also they do not want to disappoint a loved one or let this person down. Again, there arises a fear of failing and a fear of rejection.

God said:

> *A merry heart doeth good like a medicine: but a broken spirit drieth the bones.*
>
> Proverbs 17:22

Broken-hearted people face fear and anxiety because they feel unloved and alone. God said:

> *Hope deferred maketh the heart sick: but when the desire cometh, it is a tree of life.*
>
> Proverbs 12:13

> *The spirit of a man will sustain his infirmity; but a wounded spirit who can bear?*
>
> Proverbs 18:14

Fear Is Not from God

Our mind *(psyche)* can either protect us against sickness (the old cliche', *mind over matter*) or submit us to the ravages of sickness.

How does the spirit of fear work?

> *Because of the voice of the enemy, because of the oppression of the wicked: for they cast iniquity upon me, and in wrath they hate me. My heart is sore pained within me: and the terrors of death are fallen upon me. Fearfulness and trembling are come upon me, and horror hath overwhelmed me. And I said, Oh that I had wings like a dove! for then would I fly away, and be at rest. Lo, then would I wander far off, and remain in the wilderness. Selah. I would hasten my escape from the windy storm and tempest.* Psalm 55:3-8

As you can see, fear is an adversary with a loud roar, a roar much like the lion of the forest. Active at night, lions are known as the most powerful of all predators of the forest. Every animal in the wild is familiar with this most-feared predator and its habits. One habit in particular of the lion is that ferocious roar.

Unmasking the Roaring Lion

When a lion roars, the sound of it echoes for miles, and for a time, this paralyzes its prey with fear. Hearing the mighty roar of the lion, other animals become restless and unsettled. Some of them take refuge in dens, in trees or wherever they might think to escape the danger that echoes through the night. They are all suddenly on guard for what could be a fatal attack.

In this same way, fear, if entertained, will paralyze a person's life. The sad thing is that most are fearing what might never happen. Their fear is a mere projection of Satan's lies. But that projection causes anxiety, which is a severe torment.

Let us examine some key words here in Psalm 55:3-8:

Terrors means "fright."

Flight means "to avoid the problem by any means of escape: a sense of false peace."

Wandering means "an aimless movement from place to place."

Escape means "taking refuge in some temporary relief: drugs, alcohol, sex or other relationships."

Fear and anxiety can occur when we are anticipating that something will happen. As an example,

Fear Is Not from God

some people stay up all night worrying about how the next day will end before it has even begun. This is called evil foreboding, and it is an unhealthy fore-telling or predicting. Just the mention of an enemy causes some to assume the worst.

Fear is the opposite of faith. Faith brings us peace and contentment; fear causes anxiety and confusion, and the person who entertains fear is tormented. Remember, *"fear hath torment."*

In olden time, the king of Syria warred against the people of Israel. They were already ravished from famine, and now they had to deal with threats from the Syrian army. But God promised them that the Lord Himself would cause their enemies to flee before them:

> *For the LORD had made the host of the Syr-ians to hear a noise of chariots, and a noise of horses, even the noise of a great host: and they said one to another, Lo, the king of Israel hath hired against us the kings of the Hittites, and the kings of the Egyptians, to come upon us. Wherefore they arose and fled in the twilight, and left their tents, and their horses, and their asses, even the camp as it was, and fled for their life.* 2 Kings 7:6-7

Unmasking the Roaring Lion

Fear can do more than cause you to worry; it can actually cause you to question your own sanity. Fear clutches at the mind, leaving it feeling foggy, not able to think straight, not capable of making a proper decision, overwhelmed and defeated. This makes you feel like you're not all there. The result is a feeling of inferiority.

Fear will make you back down when indeed God has created you to be an overcomer and a conqueror through His Son Jesus. Fear will torment you with incidents of your past. Those incidents are over, and yet you are still controlled by their effects. The nature of fear and its effects is to paralyze you, torment you and rend you incapacitated—to the point of sickness and even death. Conquer this enemy before it conquers you.

CHAPTER 3

What God Has Given Us

*For God hath not given us the spirit of fear;
but of power, and of love, and of a sound mind.*
2 Timothy 1:7

So we know that God has not given us fear. But what has He given us?

God Has Given Us Power

Through the gift of the Holy Spirit, we have all we need to lead us to victory. The Holy Spirit, in His administration, gives us these precious promises:

*And the spirit of the LORD shall rest upon him,
the spirit of wisdom and understanding, the*

> *spirit of counsel and might, the spirit of knowl-*
> *edge and of the fear of the* LORD.   Isaiah 11:2

As believers, we have these seven gifts available to us through the operation of the Holy Spirit. We are *"endued with power from on high"* (Luke 24:49).

God has given us the power to control our thoughts, our situations and our atmosphere. In Christ Jesus, we have all that is needed to bring the enemy of our mind under subjection:

> *Casting down imaginations, and every high thing that exalteth itself against the knowl-*
> *edge of God, and bringing into captivity every thought to the obedience of Christ.*
>   2 Corinthians 10:5

Every good and perfect gift comes from the Father.

> *Every good gift and every perfect gift is from above, and cometh down from the Father of lights.*   James 1:17

God has given us a gift of power.

What God Has Given Us

Power (G1411; *doo'-nam-is*) "dunamis, force or ability, abundance, meaning, might, strength." We have this explosive force—the Holy Ghost, the promise—and it is a gift from God to all His children:

> *And, behold, I send the promise of my Father upon you: but tarry ye in the city of Jerusalem, until ye be endued with power from on high.*
>
> Luke 24:49

Before Jesus left His disciples, He promised them another Comforter. Therefore, we know that we are not alone. We have an abiding power working within us:

> *And I will pray the Father, and he shall give you another Comforter, that he may abide with you for ever; even the Spirit of truth; whom the world cannot receive, because it seeth him not, neither knoweth him: but ye know him; for he dwelleth with you, and shall be in you. I will not leave you comfortless: I will come to you.*
>
> John 14:16-18

We, therefore, have the power to deal with inadequacy and inferiority, through the Holy

Spirit. He gives us the power to succeed and excel in every area of life.

God gives us the power to transform our thoughts. Those thoughts motivate our actions. When fear comes knocking, we can gladly remind the enemy of what Jesus said: *"It is written"* (Matthew 4:4, 6, 7 and 10). God has promised us deliverance:

> *Nay, in all these things we are more than conquerors through him that loved us.*
>
> Romans 8:37

> *And he said, The LORD is my rock, and my fortress, and my deliverer.*   2 Samuel 22:2

When we serve God wholly, He gives us the power of the Gospel.

The Scriptures encourage us to be at peace with all men and warn us that when we are angry, we do not sin. They tell us that the wages of sin is death and that if we do good, we shall live and prosper:

> *Be ye angry, and sin not: let not the sun go down upon your wrath.*   Ephesians 4:26

What God Has Given Us

We have the power to make peace.

> *If it be possible, as much as lieth in you, live*
> *peaceably with all men.* Romans 18:12

We have a Teacher and Counselor administrating in and through us—the Holy Spirit:

> *But the Comforter, which is the Holy Ghost,*
> *whom the Father will send in my name, he shall*
> *teach you all things, and bring all things to your*
> *remembrance, whatsoever I have said unto you.*
> *Peace I leave with you, my peace I give unto*
> *you: not as the world giveth, give I unto you.*
> *Let not your heart be troubled, neither let it be*
> *afraid.* John 14:26-27

It is through the Holy Spirit that we produce the fruit of the Spirit, and therein, is the Father glorified:

> *But the fruit of the Spirit is love, joy, peace,*
> *longsuffering, gentleness, goodness, faith,*
> *meekness, temperance: against such there is no*
> *law.* Galatians 5:22-23

God Has Given us Love

For God hath not given us the spirit of fear; but of power, and of love, and of a sound mind.
2 Timothy 1:7

Love (G26; *agape; ag-ah'-pay*) "affection or benevolence; specifically a love feast; charity, dear, love."

He that loveth not knoweth not God; for God is love. 1 John 4:8

Love is an attribute of God, and carnal man cannot know love unless he is born of the Spirit, born of God. This type of love is only produced in humans by the aid of the Holy Spirit.

God has given us the spirit of love. Love is one of the Father's attribute. A child mimics the father, and so shall we imitate our heavenly Father. We must embrace love as our portion, our covering and our very being. Love overcomes every act and intention of fear:

The blessing of the Lord, it maketh rich, and he addeth no sorrow with it. Proverbs 10:22

What God Has Given Us

The Lord *preserveth all them that love him:*
but all the wicked will he destroy.

Psalm 145:20

The Lord has given us love, and the demonstration of this love is found in John 3:16:

For God so loved the world, that he gave his
only begotten Son, that whosoever believeth in
him should not perish, but have everlasting life.

The prophet Zephaniah declared:

The Lord *thy God in the midst of thee is*
mighty; he will save, he will rejoice over thee
with joy; he will rest in his love, he will joy
over thee with singing.   Zephaniah 3:17

We have the love of God shed abroad in our hearts and, therefore, we are confident:

And hope maketh not ashamed; because the
love of God is shed abroad in our hearts by
the Holy Ghost which is given unto us.

Romans 5:5.

God is love, and we are His children and share His DNA. This God-love must be perfected in us as believers:

> *There is no fear in love; but perfect love casteth out*
> *fear: because fear hath torment. He that feareth is*
> *not made perfect in love. We love him, because he*
> *first loved us.* 1 John 4:18-19

Each day of our lives, our loving heavenly Father loads us with benefits and perfect gifts:

> *Blessed be the LORD, who daily loadeth us with*
> *benefits, even the God of our salvation. Selah.*
> Psalm 68:19

God's gifts are perfect, and they add no sorrow with them. His love enables us to overcome the accusations of Satan. The slandering of the tongue will come, but God will silence the voice of the enemy. It is He who vindicates His children.

Love makes us confident before God and others. It helps us deal with our feelings of inferiority and insecurity. It assures us of our place in this world. We are ambassadors for God. His love casts away our sense of

What God Has Given Us

intimidation. I am no longer afraid of what the enemy says about me, for I can do all things through Christ who strengthens me.

God so loved the world that He sent His only begotten Son into the world to save us, to reconcile His people back unto Himself. Now, nothing can separate us from His love:

> *Nor height, nor depth, nor any other creature, shall be able to separate us from the love of God, which is in Christ Jesus our Lord. In all these things we are more than conquerors through him that loved us.*
>
> Romans 8:37

With God's love, comes hope. He Himself has done all these things for us:

> *But God, who is rich in mercy, for his great love wherewith he loved us.*
> *And hath raised us up together, and made us sit together in heavenly places in Christ Jesus.*
>
> Ephesians 2:4 and 6

This love and its manifestations make a believer very confident that what God has started He is perfectly able to finish:

> *Being confident of this very thing, that he which hath begun a good work in you will perform it until the day of Jesus Christ.*
>
> Philippians 1:6

Again, humans cannot exercise this love on their own. This love that is not selfish, self-centered, rude or harsh, this love that overlooks wrongs comes from the heart of God. A human can love unconditionally only when his heart has been filled with the love of God, that *agape* love, the love that covers all wrongs, the love that forgives seventy times seven, the love that keeps no records of wrong, the love that enables us to love others as God has loved us:

> *In this was manifested the love of God toward us, because that God sent his only begotten Son into the world, that we might live through him. Herein is love, not that we loved God, but that he loved us, and sent his Son to be the propitiation for our sins. Beloved, if God so loved us, we ought also to love one another.*   1 John 4:9-11

God Has Given Us a Sound Mind

Yes, God has given us a sound mind. *Sound mind* (G4995, *so-fron-is-mos'*) "discipline, that is, self-control." From (G4994, *so-fron-id'-zo*) "to make of sound mind, that is to discipline or correct; teach to be sober: discreet, sober and temperate."

The sound mind God gives us helps us deal with any sense of inaction. It gives us clarity and the ability to think clearly. A sound mind brings control, and it gives us the ability to compose ourselves and helps us to choose our responses wisely. It brings action under control, and we are no longer wandering, desperate for help, paralyzed or running from everybody. A sound mind also gives us comprehension, the ability to understand what is going on. In the midst of chaos, we are able to remain under control, choosing the correct responses and executing them effectively.

God has given us the power of grace to keep ourselves in shape, both spiritually and physically. The apostle Paul's view of a saint was as, 1) a soldier, 2) a farmer, and 3) an athlete. Athletes must discipline themselves through vigorous exercise. Their exercising must be consistent and repetitious, with the goal of mastery in view. He wrote:

> *But I keep under my body and bring it into subjection: lest that by any means, when I have preached to others, I myself should be a castaway.* 1 Corinthians 9:27

How did the apostle Paul keep his body under subjection? Here is a test using three important elements:

1. Is it helpful?
2. Is it constructive?
3. Does it glorify God?

We can use these same elements to aid us in exercising self-control whenever temptation shows its ugly head. We are capable of exercising self-control, for we have the mind of Christ. This includes His counsel, His wisdom, His understanding and His knowledge.

It is through Christ's working in us that we reverence the Father:

What God Has Given Us

For it is God which worketh in you both to will and to do of his good pleasure.

Philippians 2:13

We must practice self-control when faced with daily decision making, so that our lives can serve as written letters to those who look on. Hopefully our lives testify of the goodness and graciousness of God. We must act like and be more like our Father which is in Heaven above. This all starts in the mind.

We must have a made-up mind, and that takes self-control. We must be fully persuaded in our mind to fight the flesh and the devil and continue to exercise a Christlike character.

This is the confidence that we have in God and His written Word that brings us to soundness of mind:

Finally, brethren, farewell. Be perfect, be of good comfort, be of one mind, live in peace; and the God of love and peace shall be with you.

2 Corinthians 13:11

CHAPTER 4

Dealing with Fear and Anxiety

Commit thy way unto the LORD; trust also in him; and he shall bring it to pass. Psalm 37:5

Commit (H1556; *gaw-lal'*) "to roll; remove, roll (away, down, together), run down, seek occasion, trust, wallow."

Commit, according to the *Merriam Webster Dictionary*, is "to carry into action deliberately; to put into charge or trust; entrust."

We know, from personal experience, that after sharing our concerns with another, we are less likely to be anxious about a matter. The comfort of knowing that someone else knows about our thoughts and fears is somehow comforting. The problem is that, in most cases, there isn't anything that person can do to change or to help us in these situations.

Dealing with Fear and Anxiety

God wants us to involve Him in all our matters. With man, many things are impossible, but with God, *nothing* is impossible. Whatever is pestering you, commit the matter to God and leave it in His hands. When we talk to God about matters that concern us, we learn to release those things into His hands.

When we engage with a person on a regular basis, we grow confident in and dependent upon that person. When this happens, we suddenly begin to share with them without resistance or restraint. It is the same with God. When we walk with God and are in constant communion with Him, we learn to tell Him everything. We learn to trust and have confidence in His might. People who tell God everything are not controlled by fear or anxiety.

Trusting and having confidence in God isn't proven until you have talked to Him about your concerns and have left them in His hands. Whenever there is hesitation to bring God into a matter, it's time to re-examine your heart motives. Wrong motives will hinder your communion with God, and that can cause you to attempt to work things out in your own strength. When that happens, you know that you haven't reached the rest of trusting God with everything:

*For he that is entered into his rest, he also hath
ceased from his own works, as God did from his.*

Hebrews 4:10

Let God do it. He always has the better way because He has the wisdom, the supernatural might
and the knowledge, and He works all things together
for our good. His vision is unlimited, and He is tire-
less.

A chef in his kitchen, his area of expertise, is
hindered by a newcomer who is always adding or
removing something from his pot. This can cause
a chef to retreat quickly. He will back away from
the stove and leave the mess to the newcomer. In
the same way, God cannot work on the things we
have left in His hands if we keep interfering with
His business.

Interfering also means "meddling, interrupting,
impeding and obstruction." This explains how we
can contribute to a longer wait. We ourselves, many
times, are the hinderance to our prayers being answered. Human effort always hinders the work of
God. If we can move out of God's way and trust
Him to perform whatever He has promised, He will
never fail us:

Dealing with Fear and Anxiety

For as the heavens are higher than the earth, so are my ways higher than your ways, and my thoughts than your thoughts.   Isaiah 55:9

God has your life plan and purpose in mind, so He works things out always with that purpose, the fulfilment of your destiny. Job said it best:

But he knoweth the way that I take: when he hath tried me, I shall come forth as gold.
                                        Job 23:10

God always works according to a divine purpose:

Casting all your care upon him; for he careth for you.   1 Peter 5:7

Casting (G1977; *ep-ir-hrip'*) "to throw upon (literally or figuratively); cast upon." God wants us free from the burdens of worry, stress and anxiety. When we pray, we are commanded to cast or throw our concerns to the Lord. Literally we should say, "Here You go, Father, I have another problem for You today." He loves it, and it gives me great pleasure to know that I can come to the Father to present to Him those things I can do nothing about, those things that would keep me from His perfect rest.

In today's world, with all of its challenges and perils, without God's help, we could easily have reason to be anxious. The loss of a job, a terminal illness or an unstable economy would be at the top of a list of many concerns. As a child of God, we are comforted to know that He is the Great Provider when we learn to seek Him in everything and for all things.

God wants us to make seeking Him a priority, and we need to fellowship with Him while He works things out for us:

> *But seek ye first the kingdom of God, and his righteousness; and all these things shall be added unto you.* Matthew 6:33

When we seek God and His desires as a priority, we become free from fear and anxiety. It is written:

> *He who dwells in the shelter of the Most High will remain secure and rest in the shadow of the Almighty [whose power no enemy can withstand].* Psalm 91:1, AMP

Dealing with Fear and Anxiety

Through God's Word, we learn His ways and we learn His promises to us. He has promised never to leave us helpless in the hands of the enemy. He will be with us always, even to the ends of the world. Therefore, seek the Lord and learn of His righteousness. When we seek God, we seek His will, and our prayers will line up with His will.

Learn to pray about absolutely everything:

Be careful for nothing.   Philippians 4:6a

Careful (G3309; *mer-im-nah'o*) "to be anxious about: (be, have) care (-ful), take thought" (from G3307; *mer'-im-nah*) "(through the idea of distraction); solicitude."

Paul encouraged the Philippian church to rejoice in the Lord always. Why? Because God knows the thoughts He has toward us:

For I know the thoughts that I think toward you, saith the Lord, thoughts of peace, and not of evil, to give you an expected end.
Jeremiah 29:11

We are to rejoice in the Lord in the good times and the bad. Some steps we should take to prevent fear and anxiety are mentioned in Philippians 4:4-8. The first of them is to rejoice always (see verse 4). In fact, we are to give thanks *"in every thing"*:

> *In every thing give thanks: for this is the will*
> *of God in Christ Jesus concerning you.*
> 1 Thessalonians 5:13

Other steps from Philippians 4 are these:

- Pray about everything: *"let your requests be made known unto God"* (Verse 6).
- Plea to God for others; pray for all men everywhere.
- Give God thanks in advance for hearing and answering your prayers. Believe and be grateful (again, see verse 4).

What is to be the outcome of our praying? The peace of God will drive out fear, anxiety and doubt, and His peace will keep your heart in sweet tranquility and your mind at rest, confidently knowing that your Father in Heaven is caring for you:

Dealing with Fear and Anxiety

*And the peace of God, which passeth all un-
derstanding, shall keep your hearts and minds
through Christ Jesus.* Philippians 4:7

Jehovah Shalom becomes your Peace because you
trust in Him.

This passage concludes with the need to think on
good and positive things. Since the mind is the vehicle
which controls our actions and behaviors, it is the
driver which takes you to your destiny. To achieve
a godly destiny, we must think godly thoughts. To
achieve a victorious life, we must think victoriously:

For as he thinketh in his heart, so is he.
Proverbs 23:7

We must renew the spirit of our mind on a regular
basis, and that means every day. This is an opportunity given to each of us.

And be renewed in the spirit of your mind.
Ephesians 4:23

We must we aware of our spirit at all times, prac-
ticing self-control and making adjustments where

needed. We must be aware of what we are thinking about. Then, as Paul taught, after you have prayed, learn to rejoice always in the Lord, cultivating a heart of gratitude and, thus, abiding in the peace of God and keeping your heart with all diligence:

> *Finally, brethren, whatsoever things are true, whatsoever things are honest, whatsoever things are just, whatsoever things are pure, whatsoever things are lovely, whatsoever things are of good report; if there be any virtue, and if there be any praise, think on these things.*   Philippians 4:8

The mind must be trained to walk in the authority that God has given us through Christ Jesus. We have the mind of Christ, and, therefore, we do not fear what man can do to us:

> *So that we may boldly say, The Lord is my helper, and I will not fear what man shall do unto me.*   Hebrews 13:6

> *Thou wilt keep him in perfect peace, whose mind is stayed on thee: because he trusteth in thee.*
>   Isaiah 26:3

Dealing with Fear and Anxiety

If you are in constant worry and fear, you will never find peace. Remember, fear has torment. If you are fearful, you are being tormented. Thoughts driven by fear are thoughts generated by doubt. What are you thinking? Why are you so fearful? Trust in the Almighty God!

CHAPTER 5

Fear and Anxiety and Their Medical Implications

For I will restore health unto thee, and I will heal thee of thy wounds, saith the Lord; because they called thee an Outcast, saying, This is Zion, whom no man seeketh after.

Jeremiah 30:17

God wants us to be healthy, but medical experts agree that fear and anxiety can adversely affect you physically.

What is fear and anxiety? Everyone periodically experiences fear and anxiety. *Fear* can be defined as "an emotional, physical, and behavioral response to an immediately recognizable external threat (e.g., an intruder, a car spinning on ice)." *Anxiety* is "a distressing, unpleasant emotional state of nervousness

70

and uneasiness; its causes are less clear." Anxiety is less tied to the exact timing of a threat; it can be anticipatory before a threat, persist after a threat has passed or occur without an identifiable threat.

Anxiety is often accompanied by physical changes and behaviors similar to those caused by fear. The following information is found in the *Merck Manual, Professional Edition*.[1]

"Some degree of anxiety is adaptive; it can help people prepare, practice, and rehearse so that their functioning is improved and can help them be appropriately cautious in potentially dangerous situations. However, beyond a certain level, anxiety causes dysfunction and undue distress. At this point, it is maladaptive and considered a disorder.

"Anxiety occurs in a wide range of physical and mental disorders, but it is the predominant symptom of several. Anxiety disorders are more common than any other class of psychiatric disorder. However, they often are not recognized and consequently not treated. Left untreated, chronic maladaptive anxiety can contribute to or interfere with treatment of some general medical disorders."

_____

1. https://www.merckmanuals.com/professional

Generalized Anxiety Disorder (GAD)

"Generalized anxiety disorder is characterized by excessive anxiety and worry that is present more days than not for less than six months about a number of activities or events. The cause is unknown, although it commonly coexists in people who have alcohol abuse, major depression, or panic disorder. Diagnosis is based on history and physical examination. Treatment is psychotherapy, drug therapy, or both.

"GAD is common, affecting about 3% of the population within a 1-yr period. Women are twice as likely to be affected as men. The disorder often begins in childhood or adolescence but may begin at any age."

Signs and Symptoms

"The focus of the worry is not restricted as it is in other psychiatric disorders (e.g., to having a panic attack, being embarrassed in public, or being contaminated); the patient has multiple worries, which often shift over time. Common worries include work and family responsibilities, money, health, safety, car repairs, and chores.

"The course is usually fluctuating and chronic, with worsening during stress. Most patients with GAD have one or more other comorbid psychiatric disorders, including major depression, specific phobia, social phobia, and panic disorder."

Etiology or Cause

"The causes of anxiety disorders are not fully known, but both psychiatric and general medical factors are involved. Many people develop anxiety disorders without any identifiable antecedent triggers. Anxiety can be a response to environmental stressors, such as the ending of a significant relationship or exposure to a life-threatening disaster.

"A variety of drugs can cause anxiety. Corticosteroids, cocaine, amphetamines, and caffeine can directly cause anxiety symptoms, while withdrawal from alcohol, sedatives, and some illicit drugs can also cause anxiety."

Online information for GAD states that anxiety and its cause or causes is unknown to science. This is important to remember.

Diagnosis

"An anxiety disorder is present and merits treatment if the following apply:

- Other causes are not identified.
- Anxiety is very distressing.
- Anxiety interferes with functioning.
- Anxiety does not stop spontaneously within a few days.

"A family history of anxiety disorders helps in making the diagnosis because some patients appear to inherit a predisposition to the same anxiety disorders that their relatives have, as well as a general susceptibility to other anxiety disorders. However, some patients appear to acquire the same disorders as their relatives through learned behavior or inheritance."

In other words, we are either blessed or cursed, according to our obedience. I say that in some cases anxiety is an inherited disease, a curse that must be cast out, and the atoning blood of Jesus applied. This will break that generational curse.

Anxiety is a wicked spirit, and it is not from God. Anxiety comes from walking in doubt and unbelief. Anything that is not of faith is sin (see Romans 14:23). If we choose to worry and not to pray, as commanded in the Scriptures, we will trust more in the roaring sound of the enemy than in the Word and promises of God Himself.

The Scriptures tell us to be anxious for nothing, but in everything pray and make our requests known to God. We are commanded *not* to worry. Worrying is an indication of a lack of trust in God:

> *As for God, his way is perfect; the word of the Lord is tried: he is a buckler to all them that trust in him.*   2 Samuel 22:31

God knows and cares for His own, and we must know that we can trust Him to do this and do all things well:

> *The Lord is good, a strong hold in the day of trouble; and he knoweth them that trust in him.*
>   Nahum 1:7

Now, continuing our discussion of the physical effects of fear:

Examination

"The causes of anxiety disorders are not fully known, but both psychiatric and general medical factors are involved."

I am not a doctor or a psychiatrist, but I believe that if doctors, psychologists or psychiatrists are unable to find any root causes for anxiety, there must be a spiritual cause. Anxiety to me, is a spiritually-rooted disease that cannot be cured with medications.

God has said:

> *If thou wilt diligently hearken to the voice of the LORD thy God, and wilt do that which is right in his sight, and wilt give ear to his commandments, and keep all his statutes, I will put none of these diseases upon thee, which I have brought upon the Egyptians: for I am the LORD that healeth thee.* Exodus 15:26

In every other place in the Bible, men gave God a name according to the way He appeared to them. Here He named Himself. This is an assurance for all saints. When we walk in the obedience of God, *"none of these diseases"* shall come upon us.

Fear and Anxiety and Their Medical Implications

Later, in Isaiah, we read how Jesus was to be wounded for us:

> *But he was wounded for our transgressions, he was bruised for our iniquities: the chastisement of our peace was upon him; and with his stripes we are healed.* Isaiah 53:5

By the stripes of the body of Jesus we were healed. We can eat anything in moderation, if done in faith, and nothing shall harm us. So, it's not what we eat that is making us sick but what's eating us. According to Colossians:

> *In the which ye also walked some time, when ye lived in them. But now ye also put off all these; anger, wrath, malice, blasphemy, filthy communication out of your mouth. Lie not one to another, seeing that ye have put off the old man with his deeds.*
>
> Colossians 3:7-9

We must obey God in order to walk in His promises. Obey His commandments and live:

> *If we be led by the spirit, we will not fulfill the
> lust of the flesh.*   Galatians 5:18

Returning to the medical side of fear and anxiety:

Treatment

"Treatments vary for the different anxiety disorders, but typically involve a combination of
psychotherapy specific for the disorder and drug
treatment. The most common drug classes used are
the benzodiazepines and SSRIs."[2]

In the next section we will discuss medications.
Medications do not treat anxiety, nor do they heal
people who suffer from anxiety. They merely manage the symptoms.

Medication and Its Use

Medication or *drugs* (G5331; *pharmakeia; far-mak-I'-ah*)
is "the use of medicine, drug or spells; magic, sorcery."
Again, Medications are used to manage the symptoms
of anxiety and do not cure it. The symptoms are always

---

2. https://www.merckmanuals.com/professional

there being suppressed with the use of medications. With medications come dangerous side effects. Again, the doctors are prescribing medications to manage the symptoms, but never curing the disease."

As I have noted, existing information on GAD states that anxiety and its cause is "unknown to science." This lets me know that the prescribed medications are little more than a cover-up of the problem, only adding problems upon problems. God wants to get to the root of our fear and anxiety.

Fear and Its Spiritual Roots

Because we know that medications do not heal fear or anxiety but only manage their symptoms, we must examine biblical healing:

> *And Jesus went about all the cities and villages, teaching in their synagogues, and preaching the gospel of the kingdom, and healing every sickness and every disease among the people.*
> Matthew 9:35

Is the ministry of Jesus still active today? Of course it is. You and I are expected to continue His ministry:

And in that same hour he cured many of their infirmities and plagues, and of evil spirits; and unto many that were blind he gave sight.

Luke 7:21

In this Church age, the apostle Paul demonstrated the power of healing and deliverance in his ministry:

So that from his body were brought unto the sick handkerchiefs or aprons, and the diseases departed from them, and the evil spirits went out of them. Acts 19:12

Healing comes when we have the faith required to draw virtue from the Lord.

A woman who came to Jesus had suffered a long time and experienced great loss at the hands of physicians:

And a woman having an issue of blood twelve years, which had spent all her living upon physicians, neither could be healed of any, came behind him, and touched the border of his garment: and immediately her issue of blood stanched. Luke 8:43-44

Fear and Anxiety and Their Medical Implications

Don't settle for capsules and portions. Be healed and made whole by coming to the Father, the true Healer.

Any spirit which causes harm is classified in the Bible as *evil* and *unclean*. An unclean spirit is also called a demon. It is an agent of Satan. A demon needs an opening or access to enter into your body. Just as their master, demons come to manipulate, deceive, control, oppress, steal, kill and destroy. You don't pick up a demon by walking down the street. Demons come in through opened doors. The most common of these doors is sin. The sin can be personal or generational.

I am not discussing demons in their totality in this book. I am focusing on an unclean spirit called Fear and Anxiety. I also use the diagnostic word *anxiety*, but anxiety is also rooted in fear. Let us look at the way in which a door might be opened to such demons.

Through Rejection

Fear can enter a person through rejection, whether it is perceived or real, and the fear of rejection is the gatekeeper. *To be rejected* is "to be denied love." The inward response is fear or anxiety, manipulation, deceit, control and oppression (see 1 John 4:18).

Once rejection is received, whether real or perceived, the rejected responds in these ways—fear or pride or fear and pride combined. Once the choice is made with a response, seeds from the root of rejection begin to produce fruit. Rejection left unattended becomes a breeding ground for many other spiritual contaminations.

We will be focusing on responding to rejection in the spirit of fear. Please remember, these spirits are not of God. God has not given us the spirit of fear.

Again, to be rejected is to be denied love, and we know that God loves us:

> *For God so loved the world, that he gave his only begotten Son, that whosoever believeth in him should not perish, but have everlasting life.*
> John 3:16

We are made in the very image of the Father:

> *And God said, Let us make man in our image, after our likeness,* Genesis 1:26

Fear and Anxiety and Their Medical Implications

When someone is rejected, that person feels that love and acceptance are denied to them. When a person feels unloved by the people who should be loving them, it's a very painful feeling. Different people have different coping skills. Some will internalize, suppressing their feelings to the point of actually feeling numb, denying all feeling. A person in such a condition will reject even the most genuine of love, using this as a safety mechanism. "No more pain!" "No one will ever hurt me again!" This is anxiety and fear with some of its fruits.

Anxiety and fear bring with them other very unpleasant fruits. I will name just a few, and you might recognize some of them.

The Fruits of Fear

- Paranoia
- Envy
- Jealousy
- Phobias of all kinds
- Inferiority
- Insecurity
- Torment (in different areas of life—job, family,

health, mental, etc.)

- Insomnia
- Anxiety
- Fear of rejection
- Self-rejection
- Self-hatred

Anxiety and Your Health

Today, we have people needing medications to manage the symptoms of anxiety daily, even several times a day. There are many aliments rooted in anxiety. Fear projects into the future, projecting what *might* happen at a later date, but God said:

> *For whatsoever is not of faith is sin.*
>   Romans 14:23

Fear and anxiety are also an act of occultism, seeking and projecting information about the future from a means other than God, another reason fear is not from God.

"Anxiety affects the subacute autonomic (involuntary bodily function) symptoms. Panic attacks caused by anxiety cause cardiorespiratory, with rapid heartbeat, palpitations, irregular beats, pain in the heart muscle, tremors, sweating and butterflies in the stomach. Generalized motor weakness and dizziness are common with nausea and occasionally diarrhea occur. "

Anxiety and Its Effects on the Physical Body

It all starts in the messaging center of the brain with the hypothalamus gland and the pituitary gland. Stress triggers the hypothalamus, and it sends a message to the pituitary and the body goes into fright, flight or resistance mode. While in either mode, hormones are being dumped into the physical body, affecting the system in certain ways. The big problems occur when the mode remains in resistance.

What Fear and Anxiety Affect

- **Brain**: The brain function, confusion, an inability to concentrate, a decreased attention span
- **Head**: Headaches, sore spots on the scalp, neck and face

- **Eyes**: Photophobic excessive tearing, watery eyes, excessive blinking
- **Lips**: Tingling or numbness around the lips
- **Ears**: Tinnitus (ringing sound, dizziness, vertigo)
- **Nose**: Increased mucus, congestion
- **Mouth**: Dry mouth, tingling around the teeth, numbness of the tongue, difficulty swallowing
- **Chest/Lungs**: Frequent coughing, a tendency to wheeze
- **Heart**: Chest pain, palpitations of the heart, missed heart beat, rapid heart rate
- **Stomach**: Increased acid, with burning, nausea, a feeling of fullness in the stomach, pain in the stomach, an increase in belching
- **Colon**: Diarrhea with excessive number of stools and mucus, increased flatus (gas)
- **Bladder**: Frequent urination, bladder spasms
- **Sex organs**: Decreased mucus with painful intercourse, impotency, erectile dysfunction (ED), delayed or no orgasm, premature ejaculation
- **Adrenal Gland**: Increased adrenaline which causes increased heart rate, increased blood pressure, increased blood sugar
- **Skin**: Itching, hives, eczema

- **Muscles**: Voluntary muscles (those under your control) muscle tightness or spasms with pain and stiffness, especially in the neck and scalp, easily fatigued (tired), autonomic smooth muscles (not under your control) increased heart rate and blood pressure, etc.
- **Lungs**: Wheezing
- **Blood vessels**: High blood pressure, headaches, migraines
- **Digestive system**: Cramps in the stomach and lower abdomen, diarrhea, colitis, spastic colon
- **Urinary system**: Bladder spasms with frequent and painful urination
- **Female organs**: Menstrual cramps, PMS[3]

The Importance of Sanctification

Paul prayed for the Galatians that their whole being would be sanctified. *Sanctification* (G38; *hagiasmos*; hag-ee-as-mos') means "purification, that is (the state) purity; concretely (by Hebraism) a purifier; holiness, sanctification; to make holy, purify or consecrate." Sanctification has these processes:

---

3. From *A More Excellent Way* by Dr. Henry Wright

Unmasking the Roaring Lion

1. Through the Word
2. Through chastisement
3. Through Holy Ghost fire
4. Through trials and testing
5. Through voluntary submission and turning away from sin

> *And the very God of peace sanctify you wholly; and I pray God your whole spirit and soul [psyche'] and body be preserved blameless unto the coming of our Lord Jesus Christ.*
>
> 1 Thessalonians 5:23

What is the answer? We must live a sanctified life before God and others, separated from the world. The works of the flesh will have you operating in rebellion to the Word of God, and thereby, causing disease-producing emotions to overtake your life:

> *But if ye be led of the Spirit, ye are not under the law. Now the works of the flesh are manifest, which are these; Adultery, fornication, uncleanness, lasciviousness, idolatry, witchcraft, hatred, variance, emulations, wrath, strife, seditions, heresies, envying, murders, drunkenness, revel-*

ing, and such like: of the which I tell you before, as I have also told you in time past, that they which do such things shall not inherit the king-dom of God. Galatians 5:18-21

Be ye angry, and sin not: let not the sun go down upon your wrath: neither give place to the devil. Ephesians 4:26-27

Anger is not a sin until you go to bed before mak-ing it right. Examine your heart regularly, for out of it flow the issues of life:

Keep thy heart with all diligence; for out of it are the issues of life. Proverbs 4:23

When we hear the Word of God and keep His sayings, we are blessed. We receive the fruits of our doings:

But he said, Yea rather, blessed are they that hear the word of God, and keep it. Luke 11:28

The Word of God contains the precepts we must follow as children of God. We must seek God and

89

His purpose and plan for our lives and not be caught up with the "me and I" wants.

> *And seek not ye what ye shall eat, or what ye shall drink, neither be ye of doubtful mind. For all these things do the nations of the world seek after: and your Father knoweth that ye have need of these things. But rather seek ye the kingdom of God; and all these things shall be added unto you.* Luke 12:29-31

Double-mindedness must be dealt with through the sanctification process. If not corrected, it leaves us with sick emotions and with distorted view of God the Father, unable to manage our feelings. With dysfunctional emotions, you have a sick body. A sick mind produces a sick body. Therefore we must not be double minded.

Double-minded (G3349; *met-eh-o-rid'-zo*) "to raise in mid-air, that is, suspend (passively fluctuate or be anxious); be of doubtful mind." In the book of James, the writer spoke of the double-minded as a person with two spirits, indecisive, unstable and unsure. *Double-minded* (G1374; *dip-'soo-khos*) "double spirited, that is vacillating (in opinion or purpose)."

When we waiver in our faith, we are considered un-stable. God desires our trust. It is our trust of God that produces the peace and the love that will defeat the spirit of fear.

What Fear Does to the Physical Body

Dr. S.I. McMillen, in *None of these Diseases*, said, "Fear is a destructive emotion that affects both psych and somatic. An upset mind produces a sick body."

Fear is torment. It keeps you in the fight or flight mode so long that you eventually remain in that state. My friend Linda, whom I have mentioned in my other books, *Breaking Free* and *One Flesh*, not only suffered all sorts of abuse, but the abuse took a toll on her health. She was gripped with fear: "When will he get angry again?" or "When will he be so cruel again?" "What should I say and what shouldn't I say to avoid his angry outbursts?"

Linda spent most of her time in anticipation of this abuse, and this caused anxiety. Linda's mind was on things that were tailor-made for the spirit of fear. Anticipation of the next round of verbal abuse brought on the spirit of anxiety for her. Remember, when we project things that will probably never happen, we invite worry, insomnia, loss of appetite, fear, nervousness and depression.

As hard as Linda tried to please Joe, she could never pinpoint when her husband would go off the deep end in his fits of rage. In time, Linda began to dislike her husband because of the way he mistreated her. That dislike became anger; the anger became hate; the hate became resentment; and the resentment became bitterness.

Along with these negative emotions came physical problems. Linda often complained about stomach problems. She spent lots of time and money on the best gastroenterologist in the area. The doctor and the medications he prescribed could not heal the abuse and its effects. The diagnoses ranged from acid reflux to irritable bowel syndrome, colitis, intestinal polyps and cancer of the anus.

Linda's primary care physician often prescribed anti-anxiety medications for her, to numb her symptoms of nervousness and anxiety. But there wasn't anything any doctor could do to cure these aliments. In the end, Linda didn't continue taking the prescribed medications because she never liked the way they made her feel, the way they controlled her body. Isn't it ironic? She wouldn't take the medications, but she took years of abuse, control and manipulation at Joe's hands.

Once Linda was divorced and she begin to seek God fervently, she started feeling better, but her physical body and psychological conditions were still a maze. She began to cultivate her relationship with the Lord, but it was difficult for her after what she had suffered at the hands of her ex-husband.

For His part, the Lord showered Linda with His love, assurance and safety. When Linda began to respond to that love and to love God back, then she began to love herself. After she became acquainted with genuine love, she was then able to love others.

Linda shared with me how God had loved her back, to the point of loving her ex-husband, that abuser. She says she now often intercedes for Joe and his new family. What she wants most is for him to receive Christ as his Lord and Savior. "Until he does," Linda said, "he will never know love, nor will he ever give love."

Linda learned to forgive Joe for all his wrongs, and she walks in love and forgiveness consistently. She often tells me that her past is the path she had to take to get to this point in purpose.

In this process, Linda learned to forgive herself and accept herself and, most importantly, to love herself. She is healthy and has been delivered from all those physical and psychological ailments. God wants us healed and walking in love, power and soundness of mind. The love of God is now made perfect in Linda's life. No more fear and anxiety.

Here is a list of common diseases and their spiritual roots:

Diseases and Their Roots

- **Addictions**—Lack of love, lack of self-esteem, insecurity
- **Asthma**—Fear
- **Bone Diseases**—Jealousy and envy
- **Cancer**—Bitterness, unforgiveness, slander of the tongue
- **Diabetes**—Rejection, self-hatred, inherited disease, guilt, gluttony, depression
- **Gastroesophageal Reflux**—Anxiety
- **Gout**—Control, anger, fear, rage, difficulty letting go
- **Heart Attacks**—Fear, stress, loneliness
- **High Blood Pressure**—Fear, anxiety, unforgiveness, rebellion, stress

Fear and Anxiety and Their Medical Implications

- **Hypothyroidism**—Fear, anxiety, self-rejection, self-hatred, guilt, stress
- **High Cholesterol**—Anger, hostility
- **Migraines**—Fear, guilt, conflict with self, self-hatred
- **Lupus**—Self-rejection, self-hatred, guilt, inherited disease
- **Rheumatoid Arthritis**—self-hatred, guilt, shame, low self-esteem
- **Sinus Allergies**—Fear, anxiety, stress, bitterness, unforgiveness, self-rejection., rebellion
- **Strokes**—Self-bitterness, self-rejection, self-hatred [4]

---

4. Adapted from *Pigs in the Parlor* by Frank and Ida Mae Hammond, *Prayers that Rout Demons* by John Eckhardt and *A More Excellent Way* by Dr. Henry W. Wright

CHAPTER 6

The Antidote to Fear

For I am persuaded, that neither death, nor life, nor angels, nor principalities, nor powers, nor things present, nor things to come, nor height, nor depth, nor any other creature, shall be able to separate us from the love of God, which is in Christ Jesus our Lord. Romans 8:38-39

Love makes all things complete and perfect. In my research and from conversing with my friend Linda, I have concluded that at some point or points in her life a door was opened to the evil spirit of fear. First and foremost, fear came into Linda's life through separation from God. At the time of the opening, she believed that the way she was being treated (or not treated) was a direct result of the way the Father felt about her. That was the major goal of the devil, and he fed this lie to her until it became a stronghold.

Second, because Linda felt unloved by the Father and also by other people who were important to her life, she fell out of love with herself. She felt disappointed with herself because she did not measure up to the standard that warranted love. She saw herself as a failure, one who didn't meet the approval of the heavenly Father and who was not good enough to love herself. Therefore, she thought she just didn't amount to anything.

Third, because Linda had rejected the love of the Father, she felt unloved and unworthy of the love of others. She didn't have the support of her loved ones and didn't think God cared because she had disappointed Him. The emotions associated with such separations are self-hatred, self-rejection, self-bitterness and guilt. These three separations (from God, from self and from others) will eventually cause spiritually-rooted diseases which affect the autoimmune system. Some examples of this are: Lupus, Crohn's disease, type 2 diabetes, rheumatoid arthritis, sinus problems, sleeping disorders, strokes, heart attacks and MS.

Linda could well have made the dreadful decision to live in the tomb of her past, as did the Gadarene man, but she chose, instead, not to live bound by Satan any longer.

> *And when he was come out of the ship, imme-*
> *diately there met him out of the tombs a man*
> *with an unclean spirit, who had his dwelling*
> *among the tombs; and no man could bind him,*
> *no, not with chains.* Mark 5:3-4

This word *tombs* (G3419; *mnemeion*, many-mi'-on) means "a remembrance, that is cenotaph (place of internment) (from G3420; *mnay'*, -nmay) "memory; remembrance." Your memories or recalls can inflict fear on you too. Memory recall is a companion spirit of bitterness. Get rid of unforgiveness, and you take the lifeline from the demon of memory recall.

The love of God makes things complete. To witness completeness and peace in our lives, we must walk in obedience to God and His Word. That will keep us healthy:

> *And said, If thou wilt diligently hearken to the*
> *voice of the Lord thy God, and wilt do that*
> *which is right in his sight, and wilt give ear to*
> *his commandments, and keep all his statutes, I*
> *will put none of these diseases upon thee, which*

The Antidote to Fear

I have brought upon the Egyptians: for I am the LORD *that healeth thee.*   Exodus 15:26

We must forgive those who offend us and do it immediately, or we might forget. The price to pay for not doing it is far more costly than any of us desire to pay.

Anger is not a sin because Christ became angry, made a whip and drove the money changers out of the Temple. How we handle anger is very important, both to God and to us.

The story of the Wicked Servant in Matthew 18 tells us how God forgives us when we ask Him to. However, the wicked servant had a brother who owed him and couldn't pay and he had that man cast into prison. Soon his lord heard about this and had the wicked servant thrown into prison himself and given into the hands of the tormentors:

> *Shouldest not thou also have had compassion on thy fellow servant, even as I had pity on thee? And his lord was wroth, and delivered him to the tormentors, till he should pay all that was due unto him. So likewise shall my heavenly Father do also unto*

*you, if ye from your hearts forgive not everyone his
brother their trespasses.*   Matthew 18:33-35

*And when ye stand praying, forgive, if ye have
ought against any: that your Father also which
is in heaven may forgive you your trespasses.*

Mark 11:25

When we walk in unforgiveness, we are walking
in rebellion toward God and His Word. We are not
forgiven because we refuse to forgive others their
trespasses against us.

Rebellion is sin, and through it, we give the
tormentors rights to our life. Who chooses the tormentors? God does. Is it His desire to torment you?
No! But that was your choice when you chose to
walk in unforgiveness.

Tormentors are demonic agents. Any agent of Satan
is an agent of torment. Remember, *"fear hath torment."*

We have help through the Holy Spirit and His
grace. We can do nothing except the power to do it
be given to us by God. The Holy Spirit is our Helper,
our Guide, our Comforter, our Advocate and our
Intercessor. In Him, the Holy Ghost, we have all the
help we need to live a sanctified life. A life dedicated

to God will keep fear and other spiritually-rooted defilements at bay.

If we love the Lord, we keep His commandments. When we obey His Word and teach others to do the same, we keep spiritually-rooted diseases away from us. When we live a life separated from the world and set apart for God, the fire of God's presence will keep these spiritually-rooted diseases from us.

CHAPTER 7

Steps to Deliverance from Fear

Now the Lord is that Spirit: and where the Spirit of the Lord is, there is liberty.

2 Corinthians 3:17

You can be set free from fear and anxiety, and here's how.

Step One: *Acknowledge Your Need for Deliverance*

When we know there is an issue that is causing us to act contrary to what God expects from us, we must seek to receive the grace to overcome it. It takes humility to confess our weaknesses. God's Word says:

Do ye think that the scripture saith in vain, The spirit that dwelleth in us lusteth to envy? But

Steps to Deliverance from Fear

he giveth more grace. Wherefore he saith, God re-
sisteth the proud, but giveth grace unto the humble.
Submit yourselves therefore to God. Resist the devil,
and he will flee from you.   James 4:5-7

Paul wrote:

And he said unto me, My grace is sufficient for
thee: for my strength is made perfect in weak-
ness. Most gladly therefore will I rather glory
in my infirmities, that the power of Christ may
rest upon me.   2 Corinthians 12:9

So, now you have all the help you need to be set free in Christ Jesus.

On a sheet of paper, list all the unfruitful works of the flesh operating through you now (and that includes the spirit of fear). Examples might be: fear, rebellion, stubbornness, gossip, being unteachable or uncorrectable, etc.

Step Two: *Get to Work*

Faith without works is dead.   James 2:20

Unmasking the Roaring Lion

If we believe God for deliverance, we must do our part, working the works. What do we need to do? First, cleanse the temple, meaning drive out anything that is unclean (see John 2:14-15). Our body is the temple of God (see 1 Corinthians 3:16-17 and 6:19). Use your authority of binding and loosing (see Matthew 12:29, Mark 3:27 and Luke 10:19).

Don't be deceived into believing that because of your religious activities you are exempt from demonic influence. That woman who was overcome with the spirit of infirmity for eighteen years had gone to church every Sunday, but she still could not help herself. She was a woman of faith, the daughter of Abraham whom Satan had bound for all those years. It wasn't until she came face-to-face with the Healer, the Redeemer, the Deliverer that she was set free:

> *And, behold, there was a woman which had a spirit of infirmity eighteen years, and was bowed together, and could in no wise lift up herself. And when Jesus saw her, he called her to him, and said unto her, Woman, thou art loosed from thine infirmity. And he laid his hands on her: and immediately she was made straight, and glorified God.* Luke 13:11-13

Steps to Deliverance from Fear

Step Three: *Keep Your Temple Occupied with Power*

The Holy Spirit is our Helper. He keeps us sealed as we walk in obedience to the Way. In the Gospel of St John, from chapter 14 to chapter 15, Jesus talked about the Holy Spirit who is Deity and part of the Holy Trinity. The Holy Ghost, who is sent in Jesus' name, seals us, driving out the unclean and keeping those things that are needful.

The Holy Spirit is a fire that sanctifies the believer, and sanctification is a sure way of keeping out unclean spirits. Once you have received deliverance, pray and wait for the infilling of the Holy Spirit. The Holy Spirit is a promise, and this promise is yours to have Him as your Helper. When demons are expelled from the temple, they must be replaced with the persons of Christ Jesus and the Holy Spirit:

> *When the unclean spirit is gone out of a man, he walketh through dry places, seeking rest; and finding none, he saith, I will return unto my house whence I came out. And when he cometh, he findeth it swept and garnished. Then goeth he, and taketh to him seven other spirits more wicked than himself; and they enter in, and*

dwell there: and the last state of that man is worse than the first. Luke 11:24-26

And I will pray the Father, and he shall give you another Comforter, that he may abide with you for ever; even the Spirit of truth; whom the world cannot receive, because it seeth him not, neither knoweth him: but ye know him; for he dwelleth with you, and shall be in you.

John 14:16-17

And be not drunk with wine, wherein is excess; but be filled with the Spirit. Ephesians 5:18

Step Four: *Be Led by the Spirit*

For as many as are led by the Spirit of God, they are the sons of God. For ye have not received the spirit of bondage again to fear; but ye have received the Spirit of adoption, whereby we cry, Abba, Father. The Spirit itself beareth witness with our spirit, that we are the children of God: and if children, then heirs; heirs of God, and joint-heirs with Christ; if so be that we suffer with him, that we may be also glorified together. Romans 8:14-17

If we are led by the Spirit of God, we will not fulfill the lusts of the flesh:

The works of the flesh are manifest by these; but if ye be led of the Spirit, ye are not under the law. Now the works of the flesh are manifest, which are these; Adultery, fornication, uncleanness, lasciviousness, idolatry, witchcraft, hatred, variance, emulations, wrath, strife, seditions, heresies, envyings, murders, drunkenness, revellings, and such like: of the which I tell you before, as I have also told you in time past, that they which do such things shall not inherit the kingdom of God. Galatians 5:18-21

Now we have put off the old man with his evil deeds and put on Christ and His works, which are these:

But the fruit of the Spirit is love, joy, peace, longsuffering, gentleness, goodness, faith, meekness, temperance: against such there is no law. Galatians 5:22-23

To maintain deliverance, we must walk in love toward God, toward self and toward others, this coupled with a consistent walk in forgiveness.

Step Five: *Write Them Down*

If my people, which are called by my name, shall humble themselves, and pray, and seek my face, and turn from their wicked ways; then will I hear from heaven, and will forgive their sin, and will heal their land. 2 Chronicles 7:14

God wants to heal your land. And not only that; He promised:

For I will restore health unto thee, and I will heal thee of thy wounds, saith the LORD; because they called thee an Outcast, saying, This is Zion, whom no man seeketh after. Jeremiah 30:17

On the same sheet of paper, after the list of works of the flesh, write down the behaviors that describe you. Remember, you must be honest about your self-examination. Once you have written these down with the leading of the Holy Spirit, recite the prayer of deliverance and believe that God will deliver you from every unclean spirit influencing your life.

Humbly submit yourself to God by drawing closer to Him, and He will draw close to you. This is the help you will receive to resist the works of the enemy. At this point, you might need to spend time in fasting and prayer. Fasting and prayer and studying of the Word always aid in humbling our soul (see James 4:7-10).

Confess your faults to God and your spiritual counselor. Don't be deceived! Trying to cover your sin will only prolong the torment. God knows all about your faults, and He wants you to come to terms with them by first acknowledging them. We confess with our mouth, and we believe with our heart that God will deliver us, just as He said He will do:

> *For with the heart man believeth unto righteousness; and with the mouth confession is made unto salvation.* Romans 10:10

Unmasking the Roaring Lion

He that covereth his sins shall not prosper: but whoso confesseth and forsaketh them shall have mercy.   Proverbs 28:13

Turn from your evil and wicked ways:

Say unto them, As I live, saith the LORD God, I have no pleasure in the death of the wicked; but that the wicked turn from his way and live: turn ye, turn ye from your evil ways; for why will ye die, O house of Israel?   Ezekiel 33:11

Make up your mind to leave all the works of darkness and its master, Satan.

Forgive those who have offended you, and to the same degree, the Lord will forgive you. Keep the door shut to the tormentors by walking in continual forgiveness:

For if ye forgive men their trespasses, your heavenly Father will also forgive you: but if ye forgive not men their trespasses, neither will your Father forgive your trespasses.
                              Matthew 6:14

Steps to Deliverance from Fear

At this point I also suggest that you work through my book *Breaking Free, a Manual for Deliverance through Prayer and Fasting.*[5] But deliverance will not come forth until you have forgiven others (see Matthew 18:15-35).

If you are still struggling with letting go through the strength of grace, contact a reputable deliverance minister for assistance. Do whatever you need to do to be free in Christ.

5. Greenwell Springs, LA (McDougal & Associates: 2019)

A Deliverance Prayer

Father, in the name of Jesus, I confess that I have sinned against You by walking according to the flesh and not according to Your Spirit. I acknowledge that I need Your help to be set free. I rest in humility, and believe that as I confess these sins, You will forgive me.

Father, deliver me from (<u>name the fruit of the flesh</u>); and I release (<u>name of the offender and the offense</u>). And I turn to You and Your ways, that I might be saved and drawn from darkness into Your marvelous light.

I renounce the works of Satan and all his darkness, and I forgive all who have offended me, just as You have forgiven me all my sins.

I bind the strongman of unforgiveness, rebellion and stubbornness in Jesus' name, and I loose into my life the love and forgiveness of God.

Father, thank You for Your love, gentleness, graciousness, kindness and for all that Your Son has done and is yet doing for me. I have been touched and changed, and I have been set free. Overwhelm me with Your love, Father, that I may walk in love forever.

Father, I confess that I have sinned against You by not walking in obedience, holiness and forgiveness. I have walked in bitterness, rebellion, ingratitude, malice, hatred, selfishness, stubbornness, instability, retaliation and strife, being uncorrectable, and these are all the fruit of the flesh. Please forgive me of these trespasses and wash me clean. Purge me of this sinful nature and create in me a clean heart.

I acknowledge that fear and anxiety are the fruit of disobedience. I renounce all behaviors and attitudes of darkness. I open myself up to You for divine deliverance daily. I will put off all these: anger, wrath, malice, blasphemy, filthy communication out of my mouth, any evil spirit entering my life through fear and anxiety and all resulting infirmity. I release myself from these evil spirits in Jesus' name. I will think on those things that are good, pure and praiseworthy. As much as in me, I will be at peace with all men.

You have not given me the spirit of fear. Therefore, I refuse to have it rule over my life. You are the Ruler of my life. I take back the grounds Satan once occupied, and I dedicated it all to You as I walk daily in reverence to You and Your Word. Sanctify me wholly unto You through Your love, Your gentleness and Your mercy.

Whom the Son sets free is free indeed. Therefore, I declare today that I am set free. Fear and anxiety no longer have me bound. I am free to serve You in spirit and in truth.

The Holy Spirit is my Helper. Help me to heed the unction of the Spirit. Help me to love as You have loved me. Help me to accept Your love for myself. Help me to love myself. Only then will I have the capacity to love You and others. Restore me wholly—body, soul and spirit. Help me to leave offense alone and follow You. If I should pick up an offense, help me to release it in the strength of grace, forgiving my offender.

In the future, when I feel a need to discuss my spiritual wellbeing (as an offense, unforgiveness e.g.) I will, without hesitation, call for the elders of the church. I understand that You want me to seek help and deliverance when necessary, from the church and my spiritual leader or leaders. Help me to walk in love, being aware of my spirit,

A Deliverance Prayer

and always ready to forgive others as You have forgiven me.

Father, close every breach in my life. Seal them shut with Your love and Your power. I receive Your love, Your power and the soundness of my mind; and I will walk in self-control through Your Spirit. I declare that this day liberty has visited me.

I thank You.

I pray in Jesus' name,
Amen!

A Daily Personal Confession

The LORD is my light and my salvation; whom shall I fear? the LORD is the strength of my life; of whom shall I be afraid? Psalm 27:1

Yea, though I walk through the valley of the shadow of death, I will fear no evil: for thou art with me; thy rod and thy staff they comfort me. Psalm 23:4

So that we may boldly say, The Lord is my helper, and I will not fear what man shall do unto me. Hebrews 13:6

I am crucified with Christ: nevertheless I live; yet not I, but Christ liveth in me: and the life which I now live in the flesh I live by the faith of the Son of God, who loved me, and gave himself for me. Galatians 2:20

A Daily Personal Confession

And the peace of God, which passeth all understanding, shall keep [my] heart and mind through Christ Jesus. Philippians 4:7

For God hath not given [me] the spirit of fear, but of power, and of love, and of a sound mind. 2 Timothy 1:7

[I have the] power to tread on serpents and scorpions, and over all the power of the enemy, and nothing shall by any means hurt [me]. Luke 10:19

No weapon that is formed against [me] shall prosper; and every tongue that shall rise against [me] in judgment [I shall] condemn. This is the heritage of the servants of the LORD, *and [my] righteousness is of the* LORD. Isaiah 54:17

[I will] be still and know that [the Lord is] God. He will be exalted among the heathen: [He] will be exalted ... in the earth. Psalm 46:10

I have pursued mine enemies and overtaken them: neither did I turn again till they were consumed. Psalm 18:37

[I follow after] righteousness [because it] tendeth to life; so he that pursueth evil pursueth it to his own death. Proverbs 11:16

The Lord is good, a strong hold in the day of trouble; and he knoweth them that trust in him. Nahum 1:7

O my God, I trust in thee: let me not be ashamed, let not mine enemies triumph over me. Psalm 25:2

By this I know that thou favourest me, because mine enemy doth not triumph over me. Psalm 41:11

Not that I speak in respect of lacking anything: for I have learned, in whatsoever state I am, therewith to be content. Philippians 4:11

For thus saith the Lord God, the Holy One of Israel; In returning and rest shall [I] be saved; in quietness and in confidence shall be [my] strength. Isaiah 30:15

A Daily Personal Confession

And this is the confidence that [I] have in him, that, if [I] ask any thing according to his will, he heareth [me].   1 John 5:14

He shall cover [me] with his feathers, and under his wings [shall I] trust: his truth shall be [my] shield and buckler.   Psalm 91:4

But the Lord is faithful, who shall stablish [me], and keep [me] from evil. 2 Thessalonians 3:3

And [I] shall be as [a] mighty [man], which tread[s] down [my] enemies in the mire of the streets in the battle: and [I] shall fight, because the LORD is with [me], and the riders on horses shall be confounded.   Zechariah 10:5

All the words of my mouth are in righteousness; there is nothing froward or perverse in them.
     Proverbs 8:8

For the LORD God will help me; therefore, shall I not be [confused]: therefore, have I set my face like a flint, and I know that I shall not be ashamed.   Isaiah 50:7

Unmasking the Roaring Lion

In every thing give thanks: for this is the will of God in Christ Jesus concerning you.

1 Thessalonians 5:18

I am bold as a lion:

The wicked flee when no man pursueth: but the righteous are bold as a lion.   Proverbs 28:1

I am a peacemaker; therefore, I am blessed:

Blessed are the peacemakers: for they shall be called the children of God.   Matthew 5:9

Today I shall bring every thought under subjection:

Casting down imaginations, and every high thing that exalteth itself against the knowledge of God, and bringing into captivity every thought to the obedience of Christ.

2 Corinthians 10:5

I serve a changeless God:

A Daily Personal Confession

Jesus Christ the same yesterday, and today, and forever. Hebrews 13:8

I love my enemies, bless them that curse me, do good to them that hate me, and pray for them which despitefully use me, and persecute me (see Matthew 5:44).

I walk in wisdom. Therefore, my days shall be many, and years shall be added to my life (see Proverbs 9:11).

I reverence the Lord and have confidence in Him. Therefore, my children and I have a place of refuge (see Proverbs 14:26)

The Lord shall deliver me, not by might, nor by power, but by His Spirit (see Zechariah 4:6).

I receive the Word of God, and the knowledge of the Lord increases in me. Therefore, I am helped (see Hosea 4:6).

As I have forgiven others who have offended me, so has God forgiven my iniquity, and He remembers my sin no more (see Jeremiah 31:34).

As much as possible, with the faith and grace that lie in me, I will live peaceably with all men (see Romans 12:18).

I follow peace with all men, and holiness, without which no man shall see the Lord (see Hebrews 12:14).

I will seek the Kingdom of God and His righteousness, and my will shall be transformed into the will of the Father (see Matthew 6:33).

I will not be anxious about what I should wear or eat nor where I will live. As I seek to please the Lord, He provides for me (see Matthew 6:31).

I cast all my care upon Him, for He cares for me (see 1 Peter 5:7).

I have renewed my mind in the Word of God and now am reminded of my position in Christ. I have put on the new man, which after God is created in righteousness and true holiness (see Ephesians 4:24).

A Daily Personal Confession

I am a faithful tither. Therefore, the Lord shall rebuke the devourer for my sake, and my fruits shall not be destroyed; neither shall my vine cast her fruit before the time in the field (see Malachi 3:11).

Because I wait upon the Lord, I am strengthened (see Isaiah 40:31).

I give and it is given unto me again; good measure, pressed down, shaken together and running over men give back into my bosom (see Luke 6:38).

I abide in Christ as my Source, and I am fruitful (see John 15:5).

I have a life of abundance because Christ did it all for me (see John 10:10).

When I pray, I forgive others. I believe God hears me and, therefore, I believe I have received my petition (see Mark 11:24).

I am a wise person who built my house upon a rock, because I hear and do the commandments of God (see Matthew 7:24).

Unmasking the Roaring Lion

The Lord will keep me in perfect peace, because my mind is stayed on Him, because I trust in Him (see Isaiah 26:3).

I am mighty in battle because I use my weapons of warfare—prayer, the Holy Spirit, praise and worship and the Word of God (see 2 Corinthians 10:3-6).

I am clothed in my warrior's armor. I have on the shield of faith, the breastplate of righteousness and the belt of truth. My feet are shod with the Gospel of peace, I have on the helmet of salvation, and the sword of the Spirit is in my hand. I am praying always in the Spirit, and I watch with all perseverance (see Ephesians 6:12-18).

My God is a consuming fire, and He shall burn off every wicked and worthless thing in my life (see Hebrews 12:29).

Through the grace of God, I shall control my tongue. My words shall be in line with the promises of God (see James 3:6).

A Daily Personal Confession

I am blessed and not cursed. I am the head and not the tail. I am first and not the last. I am above only and not beneath (see Deuteronomy 28:13).

Amen!

Resources

https://www.merckmanuals.com/professional/psy-chiatric-disorders/anxiety-and-stressor-related-disorders/overview-of-anxiety-disorders

https://biblehub.com/topical/d/drugs.htm

Pigs in the Parlor; Frank and Ida Mae Hammond; with reflections by Frank Hammond

Rejection; it fruits & Its Roots; by William G. Null, M.D.

Battlefield of the Mind; Joyce Meyers Life in The Word, Inc. 1995

A More Excellent Way; Be in Health by Dr. Henry W. Wright

S.I. McMillen, M.D. *"None of These Disease."*

Author Contact Page

Jane P. McCoy
Broken Wings Healing Ministries International
P.O. Box 366
Carencro, Louisiana 70520

Phone: 337-356-1583

www.janeministries.org

Jane Ministries on Facebook @janeministries
Personal Facebook ID: Jane McCoy

Books by Jane P. McCoy

Breaking Free

A Manual for Finding Deliverance through Prayer and Fasting

Jane P. McCoy

One Flesh

Discovering Kingdom Principles for Your Marriage

Jane P. McCoy

UNMASKING THE ROARING LION

Understanding Fear and Its Design

JANE P. MCCOY

www.ingramcontent.com/pod-product-compliance
Lightning Source LLC
La Vergne TN
LVHW011334080426
835513LV00006B/344